Entangled by Nature

Jena Rose

Entangled By Nature takes people through an inner journey of the soul. It brings meaning, depth, and purpose to life and its many transformative phases. This book is divided into four chapters with each one serving a different purpose. There is a little bit of heartbreak, with some magic. A side of sweetness with some mysticism, spirituality and inspiration. It is a collection of poems, quotes and prose that have been channeled with purpose in hopes to help make you feel something, to soften your heart and guide you more within yourself. It'll encourage you to chase your dreams and see through the eyes of love more. To feel, to notice and appreciate everything around you. That the life we live is poetry itself. May this book speak to your heart as it did mine while I wrote it. May it be your reminder.

www.jenarosecreative.com
Instagram: @jenarose111

Cover design and illustrations by Lilly Prinz
Layout design by Rebecca Reitz
Book Copyright ©2021 Jena Rose

All Rights Reserved
This book or any portion thereof
may not be reproduced or used in any manner whatsoever
without the express written permission of the author
except for the use of brief quotations in a book review.

Contents

Love 7

Cracked *37*

My Heart *143*

Wide Open *205*

Afterword *241*

My mind is an unread mystery novel
waiting for pages to be read.
Come sift through the parts of me
that are left unsaid.

The mind of a writer is not organized
although it appears that way on paper.
Behind the book you will step foot into a forest
exploring their soul over thousands of acres.
Page after page
layered like a cake of everything messy.
Sleepless nights and heart aches
with their thoughts entangled with their hearts.

Entangled by Nature

I want to be like a book.
I don't want to be judged based off of my cover
but what lies within.
I want to be felt
not heard.
I want to be looked into
a glimpse into my soul.

ENTANGLED BY NATURE

So many people just want to explore
the shallow ends of my mind.

But please
ask me to go deeper.

Come get lost in the world
under my seas.

Her eyes spoke of something unique
a language to the world unknown.
If you're lucky she'll give you a peak
into a magical world of her own.

Our beauty isn't defined by our skin
it's defined by what's within.

The sunset magic begins to poke through the trees
as I gaze out my window.
The array of colors
reminds me of a heavenly disco.
The beautiful lights dance and make love
in the middle of my iris.
Captivating my minds eye
that spreads through my body like a virus.

I wonder who else could be watching
this slow motion film that moves too fast.
4 or 10 minutes
I don't even know
but they never seem to last.

There the sun goes
she's just about gone.
Tucking herself in
under the horizon.

And to think
somewhere else
the sun is already rising.

Looking up above
snowflakes fall all around.
As they fall from the sky
they speed up and slow down.
Weaving ferociously soft
in and out of the wind
they barely make a sound.

Falling in slow motion and increasing with speed.
Managing not to melt
mother nature succeeds.
The flakes clump together
leaving a pile on the ground.
To see God's artistic hand at work
leaves me profound.

The feeling of snow still excites me and keeps my soul wild.
It brings out my inner excitable child.

I dream of jumping into the fluffy abyss.
My own personal snow globe
nirvana pure bliss.

As I take a deep breath
the cold air penetrates my airways
and I wonder how long this fresh coat of snow will stay.

Snow is a welcomed visitor of mine
of whom I pray
a visitor that I wish would forever stay.

— *Snow globe flurries*

I've never understood why
but every night I look up and out at the sky.
There hasn't ever been a time
that I wasn't mesmerized.

ENTANGLED BY NATURE

Fire flies
night time sky.
Campfire ash
floats on by.

In the distance
hot embers crackle.
Nocturnal deer come out
unshackled.

Shadows are seen off in the distance from the dancing flame.
Exposing things imaginary
playing tricks on my brain.

I wonder what's really out there
in the woods at night.
Is it different than when the sky is filled with light?
I close my eyes and welcome the feel of the wind on my skin.
It picks and pulls through my hair and I just grin.

The smell of burning wood infiltrates the air.
A conversation is carried between people
although I am hardly there.
What they were saying vanishes
and I hardly care.

I'm lost in the aroma of nature
being blanketed with it's comfort.
It slowly sinks in
that we are about out of lumber
and soon the flame will be out
with the night sky, returning to its darkened slumber.

What is magic?

Is it when things seamlessly come together?
Like a rainbow after stormy weather?
Or the beauty that comes from something tragic?
Like going to heaven after something fatally traumatic?

Is magic something that is a miracle?
Or something that goes unexplained?
Like mystery and uncertainty entertained?
Is it witnessing a shooting star dive to the Earth?
Or life itself, when a mother gives birth?

City lights at incomprehensible heights?
When true loves first kiss ignites?
A raging ocean with vast depths?
Overcoming things we thought we could not accept?

Is it witnessing random acts of kindness?
Or moments that are priceless?

The point is:

Magic is not some state of psychosis
but something that requires mindful focus.
If you don't pay attention
it'll go unnoticed.

Magic is found in the present.
Magic is found in moments.

Sometimes she wanted to escape reality
to a world hidden and unknown.

He asked me, "Now that it is summer, why don't you want to be outside? During winter you pay money to travel, why can't this be a place that you can hide?"

Not sure if he could understand, I answered, "Where else could I go where ferocious waves knock over my soul?"

In the silence I was only left with the whispers of my heart.

I drifted off into thought. Imagining myself there, the only place where I feel whole. Living there someday, even if it's just a part of the time, is one of my largest goals. When I'm not there, my heart is left with this giant hole. But instead, I'm stuck here, in-between my dreams.

I want to be where the waves pull my hair down under its embrace. That when I peel myself from the water, my salt licked hair sticks to my face. Body surfing inside a swell, is my favorite place.

To witness the sun and moons romantic endeavor of nostalgia, for the times they would meet over the horizon and kiss. That when you witness them meet at sun rise and sun set, It is definitely a place you would always want to remember, never forget and forever miss.

What else do I love about this place?

Where amazonian tropical lust can river through my exotic jungle of veins? I can practice asana on the beach with my toes grounded in the sand and society can't hold me here with their chains.

I'll take an ocean breeze with a side of palm tree breeze please.

Where love, connection and peace is expressed with ease.
The people here dance and sing along because they too are under the spell of the islands song.

Just as my inner dialogue was about to ramble on, he interrupted my thoughts by asking,

"Where are the waves in which your soul long?"

With a soft smile I replied,
"That place for me, would be St. John."

— *Love City*

We are all living
 in a world
 of our own definition
  of *crazy*.

ENTANGLED BY NATURE

Why and how come?
What happens when I die?
How do I exist?
Why do I hate goodbyes?
How come love and peace can't coexist?
Too many questions to fit on one list.
Does fate exist or do we live by chance?
Why does life pass as quick as a glance?
If I made other choices
how would my life be different?
What if
when I die
it's all insignificant?

— *I'm curious*

I used to think that I never fit in
but maybe
this world just doesn't fit in with me.

She is a lover of the cosmos
and how the night sky smiles.

I enjoy exploring the depths of nature
just like I enjoy exploring the depths
of my mind.

ENTANGLED BY NATURE

I'm like a sail boat
getting carried away and consumed by what excites me
and whenever the direction of my heart changes
so does the wind in my sails.

That's why I need an anchor in my life.
To keep me from getting too carried away
and from losing touch with reality
when I become lost in my dreams.

— *Captain starry eyed*
Jena, the sailor of dreams and idealism.

I gave my life to the sun
so my heart could live under the moon.

— *Night owl*

Eyes are my favorite.
They speak in ways
that words never can.

Your sunshine waters put me into a dreamy daze.
With the sky whispering clouds above the oceans continual waves.
I am always under your spell
forced to obey your ways.
I am
your touristic slave.

— *Lemurian Soul*

She had depth just like the ocean

    who's eyes were Caribbean green.

        When he asked her what she believed in

            she replied, "I believe in all things unseen."

I love when the sky is lit bright
with flaming shooting lights.
I live for starry nights.

Sometimes

you have to chase old dreams
in order to find new ones.

ENTANGLED BY NATURE

Trusting the universe is like the scene in Aladdin
where he reaches his hand down to princess Jasmine.

From his magic carpet
he says, "Do you trust me?"

She hesitantly says yes
but as she puts her hand into his
she is brought on this ridiculously magical journey.

Even though she was afraid
she did it anyway
and surprised herself with the wildest adventure.

When you allow yourself to be seen and follow your heart
there is no greater feeling.

— *A whole new world,* here I come.

Daydreams and miracles
turned her into a believer
of unlimited possibilities
and all things magic.

Cracked

— *this is where the light gets in*

ENTANGLED BY NATURE

A rose garden grew within my heart
and thorns wrapped tightly around it
to keep anyone away who intended to hurt me
and to protect what was within.

Anyone that tried to get too close
would get pricked.
Within my heart
was a place that no one could get in.

It wasn't until I healed my wounds
that the patch of thorns withered away
and now where those thorns once were
roses have emerged.

I am Jena,
A rose in full bloom.

*Jena Rose**

**Side note* — I used to strongly dislike my middle name, but that was also during a period of my life that I didn't love much about myself. I thought most people didn't love me, so why should I love me?

After years of inner work and uprooting my subconscious wounds and healing / loving all the broken pieces that I was, I fell in love with my middle name. Along with growing to love many other aspects of my being. Now, my name carries metaphorical meaning.

I don't know a strong person
that hasn't had a troubled past.
It's through being broken
where we gain our strength.

Cracked wide open

Don't stop reading
because its sad.

Some of the greatest things in life
occur from tragedy.

You can find comfort in the darkness.

— *Lessons from the stars.*

A broken heart

               is consisted of many pieces

... and this is just one of them

I want to feel something different for awhile
instead of the thoughts
that are always trying to scratch their way
out of my mind.

Where's the off switch on this thing?

— *Overthinking*

Sometimes I experience feelings
that I don't have the words to put to.
So when others ask, "How are you?"
And I reply with, "I don't know."
It's because I really don't... know.

It is possible to feel so many things at once
that you don't even know where to begin
when it comes to sharing with others.

There was so much said
in the silence between us.

Not everyone will understand.
Because not everyone can handle the truth.

What has once been sweet
has now become something bitter.

Foul tasting to the heart.

On
days
that
I
forget
how
to
shine

the sun reminds me.

ENTANGLED BY NATURE

I witnessed you be angry
more than you were ever kind.
Happy memories between us
are really hard to find.
Closed behind doors
the things people never saw.
From the outside
people could never witness a flaw.
Your words struck my soul
and left a bruise.
All I wanted was for you to love me
but you refused.
Just another day
the same ol' abuse.
For your actions
I used to blame myself.
Your drug induced rage
I wish I could've repelled.
It was never my fault
for the way you treated us.
You had good kids
who would never put up too much of a fuss.
Life moved anywhere but forward.
If we asked for love
we got tortured.

If your heart can't carry enough love for yourself
how could I ever expect you to love anyone else?

My past and trauma may have been incredibly painful
but I love the person it turned me into.
I am the lotus flower
who's roots have grown from the mud
and transformed
into something beautiful.

ENTANGLED BY NATURE

I worried about the rain.
I worried about the lightning.
I worried about the down pour.

Forgetting my why.
Forgetting about the rainbow.
Forgetting that it can't storm forever.

Self inflicting pain.

— *My thoughts*

ENTANGLED BY NATURE

You don't have to be miles away
or states apart
in order to be distant
from someone.

When you told me
you could live without me
I knew what you felt
wasn't love.

ENTANGLED BY NATURE

Just like the moon eventually disappears from the sky
so did your love for me.

... And so did the pain that I grieved for you.
Eventually that disappeared too.

People saw potential in me
but they weren't attached
to my fears and insecurities.

ENTANGLED BY NATURE

My shadow has taken over again
consuming my light.
The darkness doesn't like anything
that's too bright.
It takes away your strength
so you can't put up a fight.
But eventually
the sun will shine again
and everything will be
alright.

— *Dusk before the dawn*

You were the one who taught me
that I shouldn't believe
everything I hear
and that not all words
are true.

— *Actions speak louder than words*

I lost my voice
metaphorically.
I was blind and couldn't see my vision.
I was starting to forget who I was.
The little girl in my heart
I allowed her to become a part of the matrix too much.
Allowing myself
to fall into the conformities
and traps of the world.

— *Remember who you are*

She said to me,

"Jena, I want to be just like you!"

I replied with a soft smile,
but thought to myself,

"No. No, you do not."

"You gotta let this go."

"You gotta move forward,
things will get better,
I promise."

Will things get better?
Or is this another lie I keep telling myself?

Eenie, meenie, miney, mo
Which way does Jena's heart want to go?

— *Which path should I take?*

Under society's microscope
my flaws and imperfections
are magnified.

How do I stand a chance?

— *Pressure*

ENTANGLED BY NATURE

I am warm in a cold place
and people try to steal my flames.

They take and they take
and when there is no more warmth to give
it is me that they blame.

— *Where do I set my limits?*

But love is hard to share
without handing over your heart.
If left unattended
some people will tare it apart.
I know you want to share your love with everyone
but your heart isn't something you can just hand over to
anyone.

— *To love or not to love, that is the question*

There are people who will be kind to your face
but behind their smile
lies their ill intentions.

— *Deceitful*

My heart is not easily satisfied.
It always wants more.
And everything ...
Eventually ...
Isn't enough.

— *Always searching*

Things were good
and then they weren't.

At what point did everything go wrong?

— *Confused*

I'm drowning
in the flood
of my thoughts.

I need someone
to throw me a raft
and save me
from the mess
that I am.

— I don't know how to swim

No matter how many people I surround myself with
I still feel alone in my mind.

She's not easy to replace.
She's hard to forget
and non duplicable.

— Her

Everyone goes through cycles in life.
While someone is getting married and celebrating their love
others are getting divorced and falling apart.
Some people are birthing new life into this world
while others express grief for a life that has been lost.

— *Yin yang*

If they know what they have done
then they wouldn't need you to clarify
what a broken heart is.

The things I want to forget
I remember.
The things I want to remember
I forget.

A dark and stormy place

— *Her heart*

The body trying to regain normalcy
after something lost.

— *Grief*

The people that thought they left you
are never really gone.
How could they be?
When they're still inside your heart.

The closer I get to people

the more it hurts

when they pull away.

ENTANGLED BY NATURE

There are two types of bruises.
The ones that are visible
and the ones you can't see.
In my experience
it's the ones you can't see
that are far more painful.

Just because
someone doesn't wear their broken heartedness on their sleeve
doesn't mean they aren't going through something.

Just because you don't see someones bruises
doesn't mean they don't feel broken.

You only know someone
based off of what they decide to show you.

— People think, but do they know?

The rain continues to fall down
on my already heavy heart

ENTANGLED BY NATURE

In a world with over seven billion people
I have never felt more alone.
Sadness runs deep into the marrow of my bones.
Tears pool and flow through my veins
where the warmth of blood used to be.
Like water during cold winter months
my heart is freezing.

I have become numb.

It's been awhile since I've felt like myself.
I am losing touch with who I used to be
I don't know who I am.

I don't know if spring will ever return
to thaw out the sadness in me.

— *A scary place to be*

It wasn't what they said that made me sad.
It was the way that they left.
Saying nothing at all.

— *No closure*

She just wanted to forget.
The sleepless nights
and all the pain they caused her.

I couldn't expose her for the monster she was without becoming one myself.

ENTANGLED BY NATURE

The way she left
was like she had vanished into thin air.
It was as if what had been
never really was.
Suddenly what they had
seized to exist.

— *Now you see me,* now you don't

She said "go"
but really meant "stay."

Just for once
she wanted someone
to choose her.

And yet I felt calm
in the chaos of my heart.

I've grown to be used to the storm.
That I didn't know what to do
when the sun would shine.

That when I finally got my rainbow
I prayed for more rain.

— *Comfort in sadness*

ENTANGLED BY NATURE

I'm not sure what it was
that made me fall in love with you.
If it was the things you said
your heart
the way you made me feel
your eyes
or the way your lips felt on mine.

All I knew
was how much it was going to hurt
when you would decide to leave.

— *Like everyone else*

40 days and 40 nights doesn't sound that bad
when compared to how often it rains inside my mind.

I've lost track
of how many times
I've died in this
lifetime.

Death ~ Rebirth

Every time my brain says, "let go."
My heart says, "no."

Without my tears being able to escape my body
I would drown from the sadness within.

"I will see you again."
"This isn't goodbye."
"Until next time."

They closed in on love
wrapping it into a hug
where tears of both
sadness and happiness fell.

—*The move*

She walked around with a hole in her chest.
She had been used to spending her whole life searching that she didn't know what she would do if she finally had everything she had been looking for.

ENTANGLED BY NATURE

Not all endings need to be painful.
You can walk away
and close a chapter of your life
ending in love and peace.

Choose to hold yourself through the grief.

*Don't define your worth
by other people's actions*

Even the moon rises
after it falls

So will you

Pain unravels the stitching of our hearts
leaving us feeling hurt and broken.

But love is the needle and thread
that sews us back together.

Love doesn't hurt us
it's everything we confuse for love that does.

— *Pain is a teacher, Love is a healer*

And maybe when we heal
we can help heal the world with us.
Rising up together.

— *Healing the Collective*

Be like the phoenix.

When you rise
allow your old life to die
with the ash and flames.
Leaving that life behind you
because your new life
will cost you your old one.

Remember:
You have so much more to gain
than you have to lose.

ENTANGLED BY NATURE

I have a difficult time with losing people.
That's why I am so selective
on who I let into my space
and who I allow myself to get close to.

Because there isn't an easy remedy
for a broken heart.

So she started again.
She built up her life
from the ashes that were left over
from the flames that burnt her.

From the ashes
she was reborn.
With flames in her hands
and a fire in her heart.

— *Aries*

Like the leaves let go of the trees
we let go of the things that no longer serve us.
So growth may take its place.

Fall is the shedding season.
The season of everything falling away.

— *Let go*

ENTANGLED BY NATURE

Forgiveness

    is the first step

        in learning

           how to trust

                someone again ...

Instead of appreciating someone for being different people misjudge and label them instead.

— *Backwards Culture*

Forgiving people that hurt you doesn't mean you're being nice to them or "giving in." Forgiving is an act of self love and being kind to yourself. When you forgive others, you remove the power that they have over you and live a life that is lighter and more freeing.

Remember

You are never too much for the right people.
Some people won't understand you and that's okay.
Those people aren't meant for you.
Allow them to fall away.

ENTANGLED BY NATURE

You deserve someone who can handle the intensity of who you are;

Your feelings,
Your heart,
Your depth,
Your mind,
Your complexity.

Not just some of it
all of it.

I am an evolving human being
who is not who they were yesterday.
I transcend and evolve
so my soul can expand
rather than decay.

For I am forever changing.

— *Life Is a Practice*

ENTANGLED BY NATURE

The leaves on a tree may change
but the branches remain.

Not everything will change
some things stay the same.

Being angry and hateful
won't change anything.

it will only take up room in your heart
from being able to feel something else.

There is beauty in everyone.
Even bullies and haters.
It's just
their inner beauty is being covered up
by their sadness
hurt
and anger.

We can't share our flames from a smoldered fire.

If we want to build up fires in this cold world
we must first ignite the flames within us.

ENTANGLED BY NATURE

Some people are only meant to be in your life for a season.
Relationships aren't always forever
everything happens for a reason.

By hanging on
you only suppress good things from being able to grow.
Like grasping a rope too tightly
you'll only end up hurting yourself more.
The only way to ease the pain
is to learn to let go.

— *Loosen your grip*

I used to be a bully to myself
getting angry with my body for everything it wasn't.
I forgot the miracle I was.
My breath that keeps me alive.
All I could think about was how I wasn't the right size
my abs weren't flat enough and my breasts weren't big enough.
I felt like I wasn't their type of pretty.

Until one day
I fell in love with myself.
Taking away other's power over me
and I couldn't believe what I had done.
I held my body tight and cried as my body spoke to me,
"How could you treat me like this? I am your home."
I thought to myself
what kind of self sabotaging monster have I become?
I spoke gently back to my body,
"I am sorry I didn't love you before.
You are beautiful and exquisite just the way you are.
I won't pick you apart anymore."

— *Learn to love your skin and the person within*

When life throws something that is against your expectations this is an invitation for you to look closer.

Because there are always hidden messages to be found in uncomfortable situations.

— *Go within*

I am a placid ocean
and even though people skip rocks across my waters
beneath the waves
my heart remains grounded and unrippled.

ENTANGLED BY NATURE

Are you really living in the present
if you're stuck in the past?

We all make mistakes.
Sometimes things happen that we don't like
but don't allow the past
to rob you of your peace for today.

What has been done
can not be undone.

— *Release*
Be here now.

Sometimes I think I don't have to practice self care
that I'll be okay
but healing and self love
is a necessity that should be practiced everyday.
It's what keeps the demons at bay.

ENTANGLED BY NATURE

She used to have a fear
of truly being loved.
She was scared to have something so good
that if she squeezed too tight
that it would still find a way
to slip through her fingers
like quicksand.

That just as fast as she had it
that it would be gone.

She was used to people leaving
not staying.

You aren't alone in your pain and suffering.

Although we have different names and journeys
we have all experienced:

pain
hurt
sadness
and loneliness.

Show people that you're human
because we want to know that we aren't alone
and that we are connected in this life.

ENTANGLED BY NATURE

Just because you grew
doesn't mean others will change too.
Sometimes you have to do what's best for you.

That's all you can do.
The rest is up to them
not up to you.

Not everyone will appreciate your evolution
but that doesn't mean you should stop growing.

Keep moving.

The committee in my mind proposed a peace treaty.
That shadow and light can both be.
They decided to settle with love and peace.
The feud has ended
and there is no longer a raging war
going on inside of me.

Sometimes things need to go wrong
in order for them to go right.

Find the beauty in the storm.
From it
is where you'll grow.

Watered down
softer ground.

A seed grows and takes root.

— *Give yourself permission to expand.*

Live in your heart.

When you trust your heart
you become centered.
The brain complicates things.
It makes you question
hesitate and doubt.

Always bring it back to the heart

Letting go of the wrong people
gives you the opportunity
to find the right ones.

I'd rather spend time with myself
instead of with those that don't value me.

— *Self Love*

There is someone out there
who has been waiting their entire life
for a love like yours.

ENTANGLED BY NATURE

The only way to get through it
is to go through it.
In order to get through the storm approaching
you need to draw the sails.
Allow the wind to pull you in.
Feel the storm as it rips and blows through you.
Feel the wind as it pulls you in each direction.
Don't be scared when the waves cast over the bow of your life.

Storms can't last forever.

— Through the struggles —

Thank you for the struggles that I face.
Through my struggles I will learn
grow and get closer to myself.

Through my struggles
I will learn how to love myself more.

When I grow and heal
so do those that surround me.

In my hardships
I give thanks.

Because through them
amazing things will come my way.

When I struggle
I will choose to imagine better things coming.

My struggles will bring me closer to my triumphs
and help me to appreciate the highs in life more.

Through my struggles I will find a way to love now.

Whether its for myself or someone else.

— *Give thanks*

Your misfortunes and struggles are an opportunity
to turn them into something beautiful.

You aren't your struggles.
You become what they shape you into.

— You decide

Reconstruction is made
from destruction.

All things can be made new.
You are allowed to renovate and remodel your life
as many times as you need
to bring yourself to your highest good.

It doesn't matter how far you've fallen.
You can always get back up.

As long as you choose yourself
you can *never* fail.

ENTANGLED BY NATURE

It's okay to fall apart
It's okay to cry
It's okay to allow yourself to feel.

Don't stuff it down so far
that you forget who you are.

You are human
just like everyone else.
Don't deny yourself
existence.

When you accept yourself for who you are
you remove the power from those who judge you.

You might be able to run away

                        from a lot of things in life

but you can never run away from your heart.

It hurts to watch you hurt yourself.
You are worth and deserve so much more
than what you are giving yourself
and I wish you could see that.
All I want is the greatest love for you.
I don't know what to do to get you to realize that.
I know you will have to find the answers on your own journey.
I know I did.
I have faith and believe in you.

Sometimes I have to keep my heart on a leash
like someone walking their dog in a park.
Otherwise
if cut loose
it'll excitably run around
and go up to things and bark.

— *Heart on a leash*

People will leave
they will break your heart in two.
You will need to grieve
in order to be made new.

Life is about finding balance.
We can't expect the light
without a little bit of dark.

Even when we can't see the moon in the night sky
we know it's still out there.

— Have faith

My Heart

Tell me, is it safe to love you?

*— A question I want to ask everyone
before handing my heart
over to them*

Love all.
Hate none.

Humans are clumsy.
They're always tripping
and falling over their hearts.

You can't love someone fully
without loving their flaws too.

— *Unconditional Love*

Humpty Dumpty had a great fall
but it was love
that put him back together after all

ENTANGLED BY NATURE

With a little bit of hell in her soul
and a fire on her tongue
it's no wonder
he's always called her
his little firecracker.

ENTANGLED BY NATURE

She's like a shot of whiskey
hot and smooth
leaving you craving
for another taste.

ENTANGLED BY NATURE

I've never felt like I was drowning
or about to run out of air
because your blue sea love
makes me serene.

ENTANGLED BY NATURE

I lay awake in the middle of the night
and although I'm almost completely still
my hair whispers over your chest
creating a small wave.

To entertain my restless thoughts
I give into my temptation
to trace my fingers across your body.

With a small touch
it raises mountains of goosebumps
that blanket across your skin.

I can't help but wonder if
you can feel me in your dreams.

ENTANGLED BY NATURE

Not even a tower of gold
the moon in my hands
all the light from the stars
or miles across land
could fill this love I have for you
that is immensely vast.

Saying I love you

is like water flowing from my lips

and I want you to take a sip.

Her mind
likes to entertain
the thoughts of him
often.

He asked her, "Why do you like the rain?"

She whispered, "When it's this beautiful, how could you not?"

—*Find the beauty in ordinary things*

Falling
    slowly
You and I
    How long will you love me?

I'm broken
you're broken
and together
we are complete.

ENTANGLED BY NATURE

And that's what's wrong with me.
I fall in love too easily.
With people
places
and experiences.
My heart is not easily satisfied
and wildly curious.

Hours
    go by
        as quick
            as seconds

whenever I'm with you.

ENTANGLED BY NATURE

Hold me
like I'm the binding of a book
that has become worn and fragile.

Be gentle
as if my pages would tare
at the slightest motion.

Appreciate me
one word
one moment
at a time.

Be here with me
and within my pages
forever.

We were

    brought together

        like a strategic game

    of chess.

Fate carefully maneuvered me through life

        bringing me closer to my king.

— Check Mate —

Your lips
traced and left
with my words
unspoken.

The people we don't expect to meet
are usually the ones that will have
the greatest impact on our lives.

ENTANGLED BY NATURE

I breathe you in
and I am intoxicated by your fragrance.
Like a spell
I am under your obeisance.

Having you around
makes me feel less lonely
in a world where I feel
mostly misunderstood.

She's silently wild.
She likes to bend the rules.
She likes to live a life a little on the edge
and he doesn't know whether that excites him
or scares him.

Run
your
fingers
through
my
soul

One. More. Time.

He has a way of calming my soul
but also bringing out
everything wild in me.

We are land and sea.
Within that space
where they both meet.

Somewhere in the middle
we are home.

Sometimes crashing
sometimes collapsing into one another.

He swallowed up my heart

into the waves of his

completely consuming me

and now

I'll forever be lost at sea.

When he came home
he wrapped his arms around her and said,
"It feels like forever since I've seen you."

As she nestled herself into his embrace
she chuckled,
"Babe, Its only been 15 hours."

He pulled her away to look into her eyes and said,
"Yeah, might as well be an entire lifetime."

— *I live for the cheesy moments*

ENTANGLED BY NATURE

If I could fall into you
like the stars fall to the earth
I would.
Just like a shooting star should.

When I look into your eyes
they are a galaxy of their own.
You and me
will always be
Our hearts
forever sown.

You have a gravitational pull on me
like the moon and sea.
Just like the stars belong in the sky
you belong with me.

I'm not sure why our passion burns hot
like a solar flare flame.

The reason why I love you so
our creator
I gratefully blame.

You are much more
than my sun, moon and stars.
You are my entire universe.

When everything
becomes complicated
he helps make it simple.

Be with someone
who will flip through
the pages of your soul.

Someone who is willing
to pull back all your layers.

She had a way of getting
into peoples hearts.

Her love was infectious.

He had a weakness
for her hands on his body
and her words in his heart.

Her heart is like
a sea shell.

If you press your ear
to her chest and listen
you will hear
the waves of her soul.

ENTANGLED BY NATURE

Enticing beauty is the kind
that makes you not want to look away.

For the fear that it may change
or it might not be there again
if you close
and re open your eyes.

He was the meteor
that came crashing
into her atmosphere
… *Changing everything.*

You give me

        the best reasons

                to stay up at night.

I love you more
than the moon could chase the sun
in an entire lifetime.

If I had to go through everything to meet you again
I would.
In this life and any life.
I would find you.
Our souls would recognize each other anywhere.

My sister: "I love you."
Me: "I love you too."
My sister: "… Forever."

— *Some of my favorite conversations*

He was the sand absorbing the sun all day.
The palm trees blowing lightly in the breeze.
The sun setting over the horizon of the Caribbean seas
and salt air subtly filling all empty spaces.

He is all things soothing
warm
and gentle.

ENTANGLED BY NATURE

I will follow the waves
I will follow the sun
I will follow the wind
and whatever else
will lead me
closer to you.

I like his lips the most
when they are pressed
against mine.

I love it when I'm feeling extra and my soul fam just reassures me and says,

"Thats okay, be as extra as you want."

Always encouraging me that it's okay to be myself.

— *Conversations with my little brother.*

When I look into him
I find myself.
When I look at him
I see me.

— *I am you*
　and you are me.

She tried to tame her heart
except you can't tame
what is meant to be wild.

Taking her face into his hands he said,

"Without you,

what meaning would my life have?"

Let my fingers trace your body
in ways a pencil never could.
Let my ears press against you
and hear the sound of your heart beating.
Let my lips speak to you
in ways my words can not.
Let me taste you
for nothing tastes sweeter.

ENTANGLED BY NATURE

When she woke
She rolled over to face him
and whispered, "good morning."
He replied by not only saying it back
but by pulling her closer into his body.
Her skin against his
and his heart against hers.

— *Good Morning*

Her heart loved him

        in a way her brain

                will never understand.

Kiss me
a few seconds
longer

So I can savor
the taste of you
on my lips.

When I look at you

while I lay in bed at night

I can't tell if I'm awake

or asleep and dreaming.

He wiped away her tears
as if he was taking her burdens
upon himself and he said,
"Let me take away your pain."

She's kind of like a tornado.

She'll come ripping through your life

sweeping up the dust in your desert heart.

Ever since she was young
she always wanted to travel to outer space.
She often daydreamed as she looked up into the night sky
wondering upon the stars.
What the world would look like from afar?
To see all things cosmic and magical
up close and personal.
It was only when she looked into his eyes
that she had seen anything remotely measurable
to what she thought she would feel
if she were an explorer of the cosmos.

She was the astronaut
who saw the universe in his eyes.

— *Cosmic Connection*

How boring it would be
to live a life
without a little bit
of crazy.

ENTANGLED BY NATURE

My heart is the ocean
and you
are every fish that swims in it.

Someone once asked me
to write about two things that go together.
So I wrote about me and you.

They found solace
in the silence of each other.

That comfortable kind of love.

ENTANGLED BY NATURE

When we open our hearts
we make room for love to pour in.

Imagine with me
how different the world would be
if love
was expressed
as much as hate.

With the colors of our skin
we make up a rainbow.
Together
we make life beautiful.

— *One Love*

ENTANGLED BY NATURE

Take it off;

Your hat,
your shoes,
your clothes,
societal roles,
pressures,
your fears,
and insecurities.

Strip it down
pull your layers back.

I want to see it all
right down to the core.
Raw —
authentic
and vulnerable.

Lead me to the path
that goes directly into your heart.

I want to see you
all of you.

When you take it all off.

And those are my favorite moments
the vulnerable ones.
Where people take off their masks
and allow you to truly see them
to their core.

If we have strong opinions and judgments of others
are we really trying to understand them?

ENTANGLED BY NATURE

Imagine how different life would be
if peoples eyes were closed.

If we were all blind.

Would it matter what people drove
what they wore or the way
their bodies looked?

No. Their quality would be based off of their hearts
and the way they loved.

Our hearts are always open
when our eyes are closed.

Close your eyes and feel into your heart.

How do people make you feel?
How do they love?

—See through the eyes of your heart

The love you give your children
is the love they will grow to have for themselves.

So love them unconditionally.

— *Children are the future*

You aren't the number on the scale.
You aren't the money in your bank account.
You aren't the things you own or the clothes that you wear.
You aren't the opinions and judgments of others.

You are your heart.
Remember who you are.

It is important to create space for ourselves to understand who we are on a deeper level. We can't just ignore our doubts, fears and insecurities if we want to move beyond them. When we choose to ignore them we only bury it deeper. Which results in subconscious wounds.

When we uproot subconscious wounds we give ourselves inner freedom and room to grow.

Your worth and how you feel about yourself determines a lot about your life. The relationships you have with people, how you treat others and yourself. The biggest critic in our lives is usually the one who lives inside our minds. Configured up of all the bad things done or said to us that have accumulated over time. Taunting us with fear.

The thoughts we have about ourselves can corner us into a small space, holding us captive and leaving us feeling small.

Self worth and self love is knowing what you deserve. It's coming home to yourself and loving all the places within your heart that maybe others may not.

To everyone reading this: You deserve love, self care, respect, the best. You deserve to be treated like you matter because you do!

You don't deserve to be hurt, not even by yourself.

We can't be afraid of being ourselves. If we aren't expressing who we are, what good things could we be keeping from ourselves? If we hide who we are, how will we connect with like minded people? How will our loving, goofy, beautiful, weird, free-spirited kindred be able to spot us? We don't want to miss out on that, do we?

We need to be the person who we hide. We need to express that part of ourselves, openly, as much as possible. You never know who you will inspire to do the same.

You are beautiful
You are strong
You are a warrior
You are an achiever
You are life
You are loved
You are everything
You are this moment

You are

When we live a life for others and not ourselves, this is where depression lives. When we are unhappy, it's because we aren't in alignment with our highest self. Don't be afraid to become who you are. When you suppress who you are, you are doing yourself and the world a disservice. You may never know who would appreciate the person that you hide. Don't rob yourself from your own heart.

— *Your true being*

I once painted the same picture with a friend and even though we were painting the same thing, they both looked entirely different.

That just goes to show how all unique we are. There is not another you to create the same art.

—*No artist is the same.*

No one has a story like you.
You are your own best seller.
Share your story.

Don't go unpublished.

I know you want to be there for everyone else
but while you are caring for everyone else
don't forget to be there for yourself.

— *You first*

— *You Are Enough* —

You don't need a reason or an excuse to feel beautiful. If you want to be beautiful, no matter what that looks like to you or how you define it, be that.

If you want love, be love.
If you want to receive, give and express gratitude.
What you want, you must first believe and feel from within.
You exist, therefore, you matter.
You are important.
You aren't "too much" or "not enough."
You are worthy of your hearts deepest and greatest desires,
You just need to believe that you deserve them.

We set the bar of expectations for ourselves by what we choose to settle with. Someone will always think you're not good enough, that you aren't nice enough or look good enough. You will always be flawed to someone. But, since when does your worth become defined by others and what they decide for you? You are what you decide to be. *You are enough.*

When you look beyond society and what others value about you, *what do you want to believe about yourself?* What do you value? How would you want the world to see you? It only matters what you think of you.

The world will adjust.

Wave the white flag
and make peace
to the war within you.

Self doubt and fear act like a disease
crippling us from being ourselves.

Every time we fall to fear
we are handing over our power and removing faith
from ourselves.

Compensating our lives over
to a murderer of hopes and dreams.

Fear is the act of removing all belief.

Anyone can literally do anything
… that's just it …

Fear can be powerful.

But it can only have as much power
as we are willing to give it.

If there is one thing that I wish I could convince people of
it is that they are enough
and they are loved
exactly the way they are.

My wish for humanity
is that people could see their worth
and how valuable their hearts are.

That they could see the good in themselves
and one other.

— *You are loved.*

No matter how hard life gets
~ don't. give. up. ~

Don't give up on yourself
or on those that are watching.
You've come way too far
to give up now.

~ Keep going ~
~ Chin up ~
~ Keep fighting ~
~You got this ~
~ I believe in you ~
~ I love you~

Repeat

Put your hand on your chest.
You feel that?

You exist.
Your body
is working hard
to keep you alive.

You are a miracle.
You matter.

Everything falls apart
so the new
can come together.

Everything happens for your good
and to shape you into who
you are meant to be.

People to love you.
People to hurt you.
Circumstances to teach you.

How else do you become wise?
How else do you become strong?

This is why everything can't be good all the time.
We have to become uncomfortable and be faced off
with things to learn and grow.
So we can appreciate the good more.

We live in a universe of balance.

The good and bad.
The yin and yang.

But it always circles back around.
Everything has meaning.
The bad always has a good lesson.
Which means the universe is always good.
So is it ever really bad?

Pain is uncomfortable, but is essential for our growth.

When you change the world within you
it acts like a ripple effect.

Rippling out of your heart
out of your body
and into the world.

If you want to change the world
you will.

By first
changing yourself.

The energy you hold for yourself
is the energy you share with the world.

It starts with you.

Repeat after me:

Self — I am sorry for underestimating you and being so hard on you. I will learn to love you more and I am sorry for all the mean things that I say to you.

— *You owe the same love to yourself
that you so willingly give to others.*

We are all the essence of love
but we somehow get covered up
by all the things that have happened to us.

— Programming

Our feelings
are an invitation from our bodies
asking us to go deeper.
To look more closely at ourselves.
To give attention
to the areas of our lives
we have pushed down
for far too long.
The areas of us
that need more *love.*

Your mind is like a sword
and to prevent it from going dull
you need to sharpen it with knowledge.

Knowledge makes for great weaponry
in the world we live in.

— I've been watching too much game of thrones. Haha

Your heart may not be understood
by many people.

But the love you give
never goes unnoticed
in the eyes of God.

— *Never stop loving, daily reminder*

ENTANGLED BY NATURE

People hold you in an energetic container of who they think you are. How people see life or themselves, is often projected onto how they view others.

The most important thing, is how you view yourself. You have the power to show up in the world the way you want to and to be the person you want to be.

You're only doing yourself a disservice if you suppress who you are because of the opinions/judgments and projections of others.

Think of it as a test.

Are you going to allow what people think, stop you from what lights up your soul and what you were called here to do/be?

Instead of fighting for the joy and happiness of others, be willing to fight for yourself.

Before engaging with something
we should get into the habit of asking ourselves,
"Is this something I want to invite into my space?"

If you don't want to expose yourself to bad things, that is an act of self love. That doesn't make you the bad guy. People are going to judge you and view you however they want anyway. You know what's best for you. Honor that. You don't have to do anything you don't want to do. If you feel like you have to put a wall up to be around someone, do you really want to put yourself into that environment? It's okay to keep yourself safe and not feed into the tension.

Honor your sacred space.

— The problem is, we think we have time. —

We are always rushing and trying to speed towards something. We get so consumed in pressing forward that we forget to stop and appreciate.

We get so obsessed with the future and what's to come, that we aren't living in the present moment, and we forget what we have right in front of us. Creating anxiety and robbing ourselves from peace and happiness, when we can find reasons to have that right now.

Right now, in this very second, this is all that is guaranteed to us. We aren't promised tomorrow and yesterday is already gone. Anything can happen at any moment.

What is something that you can be thankful for, right now? Slow your mind, eliminate the clutter and observe. What's something you can appreciate? Who could you hug, or remind them of how much they are loved? What is something you can be happy about? What do you have that makes you blessed?

ENTANGLED BY NATURE

Just in case if no one has told you today:

I love you.

I love you today and tomorrow.
In this moment and every moment there after.
As long as I'm breathing and am alive
I will love you.

We all deserve to be loved
and to know that we are loved.

I may not know you
but that doesn't mean
that I can't still love you.

Afterword

---♦---

My hope for you is that you will feel this love and carry it with you. I hope my words have touched a place in your heart because all I want to do is to help be a beacon for others and to shine a light on a path for everyone. You aren't alone in your pain and suffering. I used to starve my heart of love when it was something I could've given myself, but I felt so undeserving of it. It wasn't until I allowed myself to be cracked wide open. It wasn't until I went within myself that I was able to see what a light I truly am and so are you!

It's important to keep our hearts open and soft and to realize that we all have suffered from something. We have all made mistakes. We have all experienced pain, loss and loneliness. We aren't that different from each other.

We are continuously searching for something to fill the gaps within us. When these gaps can only be filled and mended with love. Love from God / Source and love for self.

I invite you to look into your life and to appreciate the beautiful human that you are. The next time that you look in the mirror, I want you to make eye contact with your soul, wrap your arms around yourself and love every inch of who you are and say out loud, "I love you. I love you so much."

That love, happiness and freedom you desire so much is within you. Love yourself and free yourself of your past and the things that have happened to you.

Making this earth a better place starts with ourselves.
When we heal ourselves, we help others heal.
When we help others heal, we heal as a collective. As a whole.

Raising the consciousness of the entire planet. Together,
we rise.

You are who you decide to be.
Don't allow people's negativity to hold a cloud over you.

Love doesn't give up, it keeps going and it is the essence of
what got you here. You are created from love. We are made
from the same spark of life.

Together
we are connected.
Together
we are love.

All the hugs and snugs

Namasté,
Jena Rose

www.ingramcontent.com/pod-product-compliance
Lightning Source LLC
Chambersburg PA
CBHW051355290426
44108CB00015B/2027